Dyslexia Rules!

An **Activity Book** of basic lessons for
severe reading and spelling disability

by Mary Manning-Thomas
illustrated by Rosie Brooks

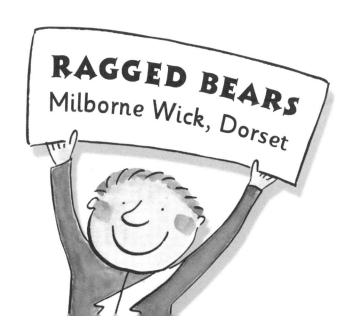

RAGGED BEARS
Milborne Wick, Dorset

Contents

Foreword

I was lucky enough to be put in touch with Mary Manning-Thomas when I realised my son was having problems with his reading and spelling. Though she had been officially 'retired' for years, in her mid-eighties, Mary was still seeing the occasional child, when referred by a friend. Felix, my son, was one of these lucky children, and the difference Mary's lessons made to his confidence was incredible, in both reading and spelling. As a parent I felt very fortunate to be given Mary's lesson plans as they were the only practical tools I had come across that could help my son.

Felix was one of the last children to meet and be assessed by Mary. Since she first started working with children with severe reading and spelling difficulties, at the West End Hospital in war-torn London in the 1940s, literally thousands of children have met and worked with her and had their lives changed. When Mary first started working with children, the condition that is now known as dyslexia was not even officially recognised, and it was Mary and the other professionals around her that proved that the condition existed all those years ago.

Mary is in her late eighties and, while her mind is active, she is physically unable to get around, so her days of travelling around the world and lecturing students or meeting children who need her help are over. Her greatest frustration is that she will never reach those children and her lessons, compiled and revised over the years, will be lost. This is the reason why she has allowed me to publish her lesson plans, so that even if she is unable to carry on her wonderful work, parents and children can still have access to her lessons, which really do make such a difference.

Henrietta S.

Henrietta Stickland
Publisher

Introduction

After helping thousands of dyslexic children over several decades through the terrible maze and vagaries of English spelling, and having studied various spelling manuals on the market, I began to realise the need for a much more basic set of useful words and exercises for children with reading and spelling difficulties to learn and to have for reference.

This book is made up of words that the children I taught over the years had difficulty with time and time again. To help your child improve their spelling and gain confidence I have listed these words in a number of lessons. I have also produced flash cards of the words found in the lessons for you to cut out of the book to help your child further. The words at the back of this book should be learned and revised again and again. The way I have suggested doing it not only acts as a learning challenge but is fun too!

Mary Manning-Thomas

The lesson plan

This book is derived from a set of 16 lessons and is easy to use. The lessons themselves are divided into three parts and should only take half an hour, giving 10 minutes to each section. At the back of the book, there are a series of words that need to be learnt for each lesson. These words should be cut out and used whilst studying the appropriate lesson.

1 Learn the spelling pattern and rule, if there is one, of the first set of words.

2 Learn the words in each lesson on a 'Look and Say' basis, by the method described on the right.

3 Each lesson has a variety of sentences to read that are appropriate to the words learnt for that particular lesson. Read each sentence aloud in turn. Now cover the sentences and ask your child to write them down, one at a time, from memory.

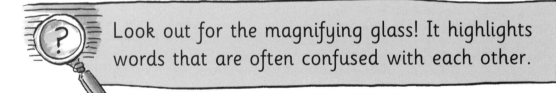 Look out for the magnifying glass! It highlights words that are often confused with each other.

Constant revision of each lesson will be needed, but only you will be able to gauge this by evaluating your child's written work. From my experience, I find this is continually needed in the early stages but it can be fun, especially if you yourself can think of some interesting variations. Remember to use humour as much as possible – revise previous lessons by using simple, short and amusing dictations such as the examples at the back of the book (see page 56). Such word play will make the whole process much more appealing to your child. Remember, as confidence is gained and sequencing ability trained, your child's progress will quicken and new words will be learnt more easily.

How to use the flash cards at the back of the book

Cut out the flash cards that relate to the lesson you are studying. Choose a flash card and hold it up for a couple of minutes while you repeat the word several times over. Now show your child how it can be divided syllabically, then spelt out, then 'photographed' – to retain the visual pattern mentally – before your child is asked to write it down immediately the card is removed. Then lay the card, plus 3 to 6 other cards, out on the table. Ask your child to hand back the word they have just learnt and to spell it aloud to you as they do so. Repeat this process several times. This method is called '**Look and Say**'.

By this method children do not realise they are reading and it can be made a lot of fun, which encourages attention and retention and caters for their combined visual and auditory retention difficulties.

You can further support your child by asking them to spell out the letters of the word you've said to them, using the cut out letters at the back of the book. Once the child has spelt the word, re-shuffle the letters and repeat the process several times. **Repetition is a powerful aid to learning!**

Another idea is to buy some magnetic letters and put them on the fridge. Choose a word you want your child to spell, mix it up with several other letters and ask them to find the right letters that spell the word you've chosen. **Making lessons fun is key to learning!**

Before you start the lessons

Circle those sounding the same in the same colour, **e.g. ee/ea**.

oo

moon

hoop

soon

room

spoon

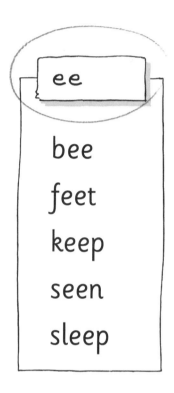

ee

bee

feet

keep

seen

sleep

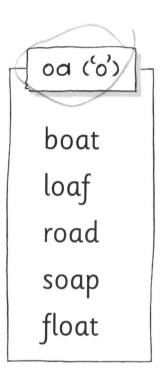

oa ('o')

boat

loaf

road

soap

float

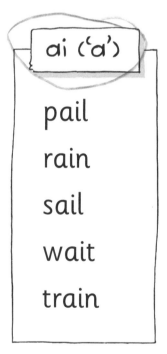

ai ('a')

pail

rain

sail

wait

train

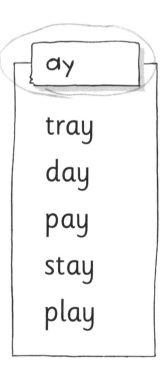

ay

tray

day

pay

stay

play

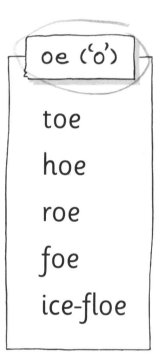

oe ('o')

toe

hoe

roe

foe

ice-floe

This exercise will help you understand how well your child hears the different sounds that certain letters make. Being able to differentiate between these sounds is a key aspect of reading and writing.

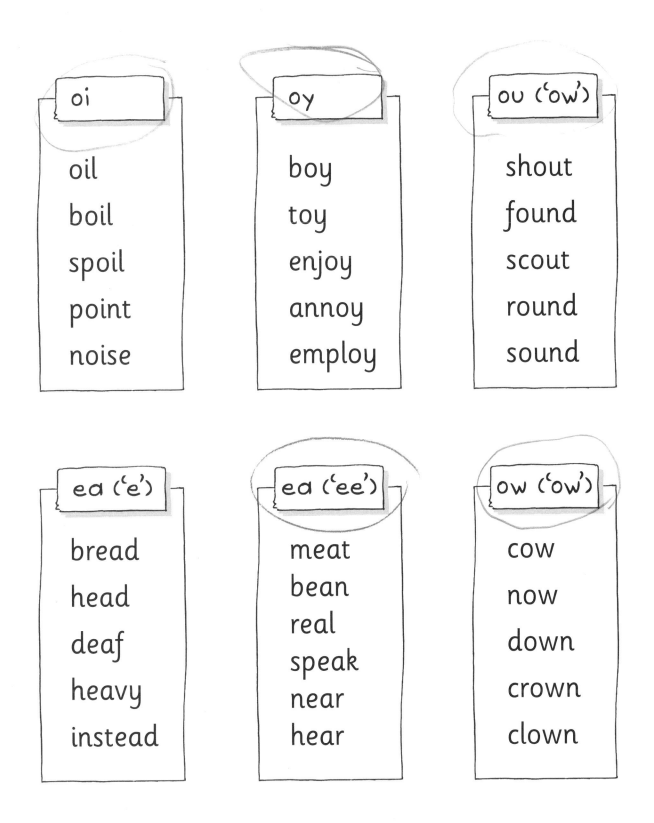

oi

oil

boil

spoil

point

noise

oy

boy

toy

enjoy

annoy

employ

ou ('ow')

shout

found

scout

round

sound

ea ('e')

bread

head

deaf

heavy

instead

ea ('ee')

meat

bean

real

speak

near

hear

ow ('ow')

cow

now

down

crown

clown

Lesson 1

Add an **'e'** and make the first vowel say its own name. For instance, the letter 'a' says its own name in the word 'rate' but not in 'rat'.

rat	rate	'a'
mad	made	'a'
rod	rode	'o'
can	cane	'a'
sit	site	'i'
rot	rote	'o'
mat	mate	'a'
bit	bite	'i'
tub	tube	'u'
cub	cube	'u'

More Words to Learn

pine	lone	pane		care	bore
fine	cone	vane		dare	wore
line	done*	mane		stare	store
	gone*	crane		bare	core

*We say these differently.

10

The boy rode his bike.

Make the tube stand
by the cube.

The cat sits on the site
of their old house.

The rat took a bite out
of the cane chair.

He made a box
out of pine wood.

It was a fine day as they
set out down the lane.

Learn

- Get your child to spell out the words for numbers one to twenty, using the letter flash cards at the back of the book.

Lesson 1a

Double the consonant before adding **-ing** . . .

stop   stopping

run   running

tap   tapping

bob   bobbing

sit   sitting

. . . but only one consonant if the vowel says its own name.

hope	hoping	'o'	hopping
cane	caning	'a'	canning
tape	taping	'a'	tapping

If you can remember this rule, your spelling life will be much easier!

Lesson 2

A word ending in **-tion** is a 'chunk' ending.

station

proportion

vocation

ration

suction

fraction

direction

vacation

adaptation

fiction

motion

lotion

nation

conviction

partition

section

erection

adoption

auction

creation

function

portion

More Words to Learn

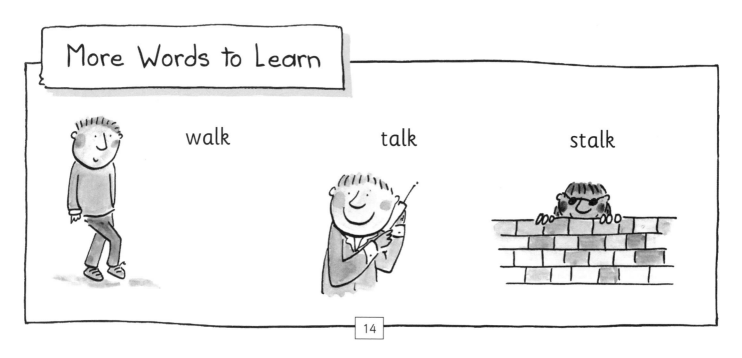

walk

talk

stalk

The station has ceased to function since Christmas.

He asked in which direction was the auction.

He went on vacation as soon as the fraction project was over.

He looked for a book of fiction in the wrong section.

The nation made a rapid adaptation to the war.

The octopus held onto the page by suction.

Revise:
Lesson 1

• Continue with words for numbers, thirty to a hundred.

Lesson 3

Words ending with **-ture** – another 'chunk' ending.

miniature

picture

mixture

nature

feature

caricature

posture

capture

overture

fixture

puncture

creature

pasture

furniture

rapture

mature

venture

adventure

More Words to Learn

palm	might	story
calm	sight	pretty
psalm	light	county
balm	knight	country

The picture fell off
its fixture.

He had a puncture
in his front tyre.

The furniture was a
mixture of new and old.

The rapture on his face showed
in every feature.

The wandering creature was found on Tom's pasture.

The artist tried to capture the posture of the model.

She lived in the
prettiest county
in the country.

Revise:
Lessons 1 and 2

• Continue to
practise numbers.

Lesson 4

Words ending in **-le**

bottle

needle

stable

rubble

marble

table

cradle

people

enable

ladle

feeble

cable

wheedle

able

muddle

rumble

scrabble

bobble

treadle

angle

angel

More Words to Learn

could
should
would

fright
night
right
fight

money
honey
donkey
monkey

The bottle was
on the table.

He was able to
play Scrabble.

She wheedled him into
cabling the money.

The marble was broken
into rubble.

The bobbles went up and
down on the cradle.

She could not find a needle
in the muddle.

Revise:
Lesson 3

Lesson 5

Soft **c** = 's' sound, *e.g. **ci/ce/cy***

city	ceiling	race	defiance
civic	certain	dance	scarce
civil	circus	office	advice
citizen	circle	service	decide
citadel	circular	police	association
cinema			anticipate
civility			
cine camera			

cycle   bi-cycle
        tri-cycle

cede   re-cede
       pre-cede
       con-cede
       pro-ceed

ci
ce = 's' sound
cy

More Words to Learn

old	gold	sold	many
cold	told	hold	any

The circus would visit the city on Thursday.

The cinema had a circular ceiling.

We must not cycle through the civic car park.

They were not certain that the circle was complete.

The citizens went to the citadel.

We should be civil to one another.

Revise:
Lessons 3 and 4

Lesson 6

Words using **-ou** (Please notice the different pronunciations.)

through   plough

            thorough   bough

though

                                             cough

thought   thoroughfare   trough

throughout   enough   rough

                                            tough

More Words to Learn

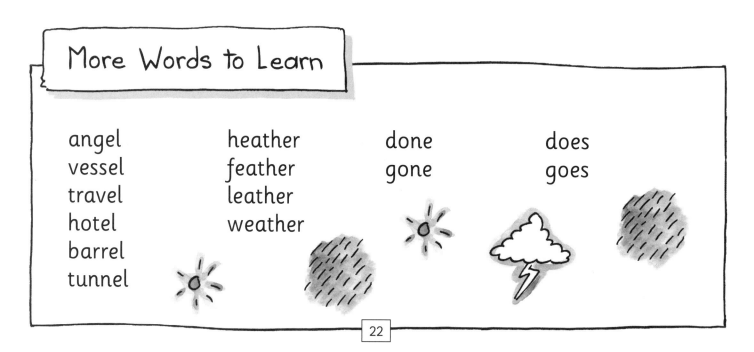

angel	heather	done	does
vessel	feather	gone	goes
travel	leather		
hotel	weather		
barrel			
tunnel			

He went through the cinema notices.

I thought he could not come to the city with his camera.

I mended my puncture even though it was so cold.

The palace had marble and gold throughout.

He gave the bottles a thorough wash-out.

He walked towards the city thoroughfare.

He caught the plough on the horse trough.

The boy thought he was tough, but we knew he was just being rough.

Revise:
Lesson 5

Lesson 7

Beat out the syllables.

be-au-ti-ful	beautifully	beauty	
be-cause	difficult	different	
usual	unusual	usually	casual
many	any	anyhow	really
useful	usefully	use	misuse
necessary	happened	several	
disappoint	suddenly	opportunity	

More Words to Learn

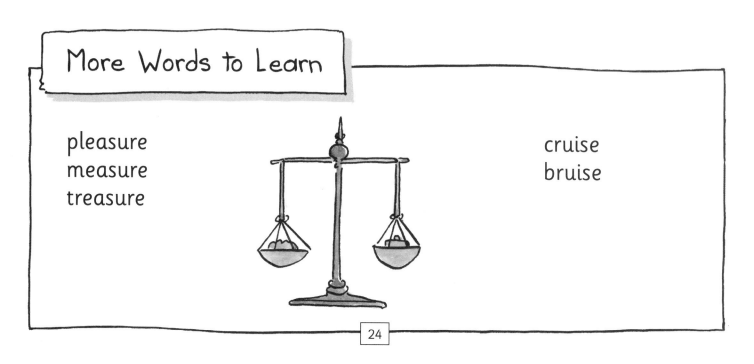

pleasure
measure
treasure

cruise
bruise

It was a calm day for a picnic and many people were disappointed when it began to rain.

He rode through the beautiful city and saw a proportion of its treasures.

They were able to see the poor creature in the stable in spite of the partition.

He made a trip to the cinema because he had been told that the film would show an interesting feature.

Revise:
Lessons 4, 5 and 6

Lesson 8

Question words beginning with '**wh**'

who?   what?   when?

where?   why?   whom?

whether?   whither?   whoever?

whatever?   whenever?

Other words beginning with '**wh**'

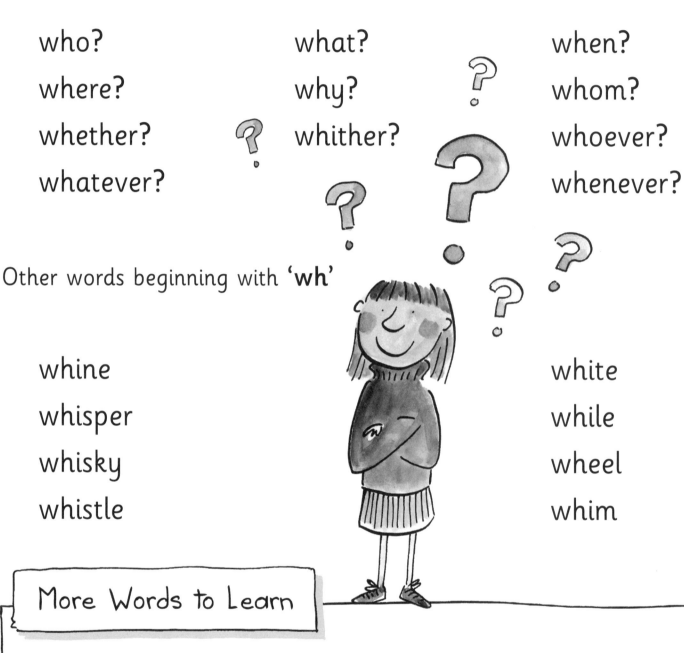

whine   white

whisper   while

whisky   wheel

whistle   whim

More Words to Learn

smoulder   shoulder   boulder

When will you know
where they are going?

Why did you paint the
wheels white?

Who will whistle for
the whining dog?

What do you think
they were doing?

When we went to
the seaside I went
swimming.

when/went

To whom shall we send the whisky?

How can I hear while you keep whispering?

The fire was smouldering.

He patted me on the shoulder.

The big boulder fell from the cliff.

Revise:
Lesson 7

Lesson 9

Words with **-au** in the middle. (Please notice the different sounds the words make.)

caught

taught

sausages

gaudy

aunt

Australia

Austria

author

autumn

August

laughter

daughter

slaughter

naughty

sauce

saucy

raucous

saucer

More Words to Learn

there (place and statement)   – over there

their (belonging to them)   – their books

They caught the
naughty boy.

Don't laugh at
my daughter.

Measure out a
pound and a half
of sausages.

What treasure did you
find in the leather trunk?

It was a pleasure to
see fine weather.

I taught the saucy boy a lesson.

Revise:
Lessons 7 and 8

Lesson 10

Some words for relations and people around us.

father	sister	neighbour
aunt	son	alien
uncle	daughter	foreigner
niece	godmother	grandpa
nephew	parent	grandma
brother		
mother		

More Words to Learn

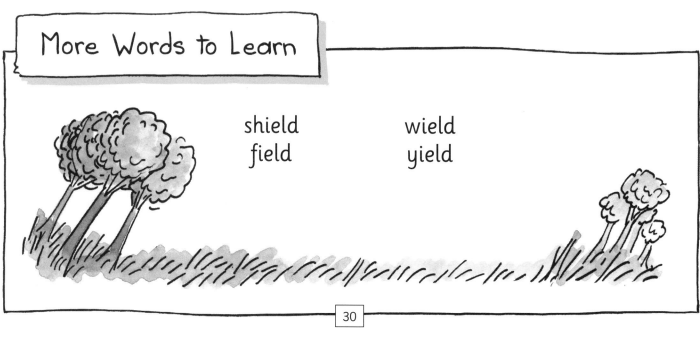

shield   wield
field   yield

My son and daughter
went to see their
aunt and uncle.

His godmother
was a foreigner.

I gave presents to my
niece and nephew.

My parents saw my sister
in the pleasure ground.

The leather books were
found in the field.

I looked at an old
shield in the museum.

Revise:
Lesson 9

Lesson 11

Words with **-or** at the end

motor	mentor	rector
tractor	sailor	mirror
factor	major	doctor
proctor	pastor	author
		terror

More Words to Learn

ought
bought
sought
brought

sulk
hulk
bulk

The doctor and the rector are important in village life.

The tractor has become a major factor in life on the farm.

The sailor told the author a tale of terror.

I ought not to have bought that mirror.

They brought the bulk of the timber on Tuesday.

The pirate sought in vain for the treasure in the old hulk of a boat.

Revise:
Lesson 10

- Read some of the sentences from the previous lessons and ask your child to write them down.

Lesson 12

Words with an **-ear** in them

heart	search	fear
heard	beard	dear
learn	earn	rear
		pear
		near

Silent Letters

kn-	knew	-mb	comb
	knee		bomb
	knight		lamb
	knife		thumb
	know		plumb (plumber)
	knock		crumb
	knowledge		climb
			dumb
-mn	autumn		tomb
	solemn		succumb
	column		
	condemn		

They searched for the
man with the beard.

He heard that he could
earn a pound picking fruit.

I knew I could learn it
by heart if I tried.

 With my comb
and some paper
held up by my
thumb, I can
make a tune.

Where did you learn all that knowledge about climbing?

I know I lost my knife near the pear tree.

The column of soldiers marched without
stopping for several hours.

Revise:

- Revise all previous lessons by writing the words and sentences again to dictation. Keep a record of how many your child gets correct each time.

Lesson 13

Words with a soft **g** at the beginning/middle/end of the word

germ	page	arranging
gym	edge	managed
gentle	strange	courageous
ginger	large	danger
gist	advantage	manager
gender	damage	menagerie

More Words to Learn

bruise   fruit   build
cruise   suit   juice

The circus manager asked the gentleman to leave as the lion had become dangerous.

The burglar took advantage of the damaged door to enter the house.

A large ginger cat sat on the edge of the sofa.

A strange germ affected the animals in the menagerie.

They ate tropical fruit on their summer cruise and enjoyed the juice.

Revise:
Lessons 10 and 11

Lesson 14

Words using the hard **ch** (k)

chord

choir

chemist

Christmas

character

chronic

chasm

technical

architect

mechanic

stomach

echo

orchestra

scheme

More Words to Learn

doubt
debt

league
vague
tongue

BILL

The chemist was not open at Christmas.

There was chaos near the chasm after the train accident.

He had chronic pain in his stomach.

A mechanic must have good technical knowledge.

He thought up a new scheme for the orchestra.

The architect joined the church choir.

Things to do:

- Use the Finish the Story dictations (see page 56) for fun revision.

Lesson 15

Words using **-us -ous -ious**

crocus	famous	various
focus	enormous	cautious
discus	fabulous	mysterious
cactus	numerous	curious
	dangerous	infectious

More Words to Learn

miscellaneous

courageous

The famous actress got a fabulous welcome.

The enormous lorry was dangerous on the narrow road.

Their various costumes looked curious in the photograph.

You must be cautious as there are numerous jellyfish in the water.

Revise:
Lessons 12, 13 and 14

Lesson 16

Words with more **'chunk'** endings

-tial

initial

substantial

essential

partial

impartial

industrial

-cial

social

racial

special

artificial

official

commercial

Read the Sentences

A substantial amount of revision is essential before examinations.

An official suggested a special artificial leg for the injured man.

-tious

-cious

pretentious

ambitious

superstitious

infectious

cautious

conscientious

precious

spacious

delicious

conscious

suspicious

vicious

Read the Sentences

I had to be cautious in case their illness was infectious.

Her precious recipe was for a delicious pudding.

The employer was conscious that the man was ambitious.

Extra Learning Fun

You'll need to make flash cards for yourself in this section! There are some blank ones at the back of the book.

Alphabet (26 letters)

Learn one line at a time to make a 'jingle'

A B c d E f g

A	B	C	D	E	F	G
a	b	c	d	e	f	g

H	I	J	K	L	M	N
h	i	j	k	l	m	n

O	P	Q	R	S	T	U
o	p	q	r	s	t	u

V	W	X	Y	Z
v	w	x	y	z

Days (7)

Monday
Tuesday
Wednesday
Thursday
Friday
Saturday
Sunday

Months (12)

Learn in threes.

January	April	July	October
February	May	August	November
March	June	September	December

Common words

Common words of the same sound, but with different spellings for different meanings.

Get your child to learn the words below in groups. Now make some cards for yourself and write the words on them. Ask your child to hand back the appropriate card when you give them the meaning in a sentence, **e.g. the trees were bare**.

pear	bear	hear	fear	beach
peer	beer	hair	fair	beech
pair	bare	hare	fare	
pier	bier	here	fir	
pare		heir*	fur	

stare	tear	rear	leek	fowl
steer	tare	rare	leak	foul
stair	tier			

Draw small pictures to help with the meanings if necessary.

*Note that the 'h' is silent.
See the following page for more examples of silent letters.

Silent letters

Make cards of the following words and get your child to learn them.

wr-	silent t	silent l
write	listen	psalm
wrong	castle	calm
wrist	whistle	half
wring	bustle	almond
wreck	hasten	salmon
wrath	fasten	calves
wriggle		calf
wreath		halves

-gue	gu-	-q
vague	guilty	antique
rogue	guess	unique
catalogue	guide	technique
intrigue	guard	
	guarantee	
	guitar	

kn-

knife
knight
knowledge
knit
knocker
knot
knee
know

silent h

rhyme
rhythm
thames
Thomas
rhinoceros
rheumatism
rhubarb

-mb

climb
thumb
lamb
comb
limb
bomb
numb
tomb
dumb

h-

honest
honour
hour
heir

gh-

ghastly
ghost
ghetto

gn-

gnaw
gnu
gnat
gnome

-bt

doubt
debt

-gn

sign
design
foreign
reign
sovereign

-mn

solemn
column
autumn
damn
condemn
hymn

Other constant confusions

Make cards of the following words and learn them the same way as before.

to	of	for	ever	either
two	off	form	every	neither
too		from	very	

left	was	court	county	dye
felt	saw	caught	country	die

rough	straight	flew	us	quite
tough	strait	flu	use	quiet

dew	mettle	on	were	idle
due	metal	no	wear	idol

forth	diary	principle	stationery	antic
fourth	dairy	principal	stationary	antique

Now get your child to:
- read the words;
- write them down as you read them aloud;
- put them into sentences themselves;
- put a ring round the silent letter in one of the words in each column.

Difficult but useful words to read and learn to spell

Look, consider, cover and write from memory. Spell aloud in groups of 2/3 letters. 'Say the beats' of longer words first.

a. after
   ache
   adequate
   adhere
   any
   acre
   association
   accident
   area
   awful
   astronaut
   aloof
   annihilation
   assailant
   accompaniment
   applaud
   authoritative
   against
   antique

b. breakfast
   build
   because
   business
   bulk
   buoyancy
   beautiful
   base
   before
   bicycle
   booty
   busy
   boulder
   burst

c. cereal
   column
   correct
   carriage
   courteous
   chauffeur
   cease
   culminate
   cough
   concrete
   carburettor
   clutch
   chest of drawers
   cupboard
   certain
   castle
   cousin
   couple
   conscience

d.
distinguish
deliberate
dormitory
desperate
design
decide
debt
doubt
disguise
discipline
dough
difficult
dirty
dubious
dissect
distance

e.
electricity
European
enough
exile
emblazon
early
eyrie
ecstasy
experience
excite
excusable
emporium
energy
every
earn
either
equal

f.
front
friend
frontier
few
fatigue
fierce
fantastic
foreign
fasten
folk
first
further
field

g.
gaiety
gasp
guide
gradient
giraffe
gear
grimace
gaily
guarantee
goal

h.
huge
hatred
half
heart
hasten
heard
heir
honour

i.
initiate
impressive
impertinence
inquisitive
imitate
island
injure
increase
important

j.	judge	k.	knight	l.	leisure
	journey		knife		level
	jubilant		knowledge		lurk
	justice		know		lemonade
	jury				learn
					listen
					laugh

m.	mechanical	n.	neighbour	o.	origin
	mechanism		nearly		orchestra
	monotonous		niece		ocean
	meringue		nice		obstinate
	menagerie		nurture		once
	moustache		neon		one
	miniature		nerves		often
	mirth		nuisance		ochre
	mourn		neurotic		ounce
	municipal		nevertheless		occur
	massive				
	mutiny				
	massacre				
	mood				
	memento				
	machine				

p. parallel
    people
    plenty
    palm
    purpose
    precious
    pneumatic
    pout
    pour
    palatial
    panorama
    precise
    pompous
    passenger
    precinct
    probable
    potential
    portrait
    perceive
    police
    plaice
    profile
    prolong
    possible
    pierce

q. quay
    queue
    quite
    quiet
    quiz
    quest

r. rhythm
    reasonable
    religious
    resin
    reconnoitre
    reverie
    routine
    retinue
    rein
    rapidly
    recruit
    rival
    realm
    receipt
    rotten
    resident
    rhyme

s. sugar
    science
    scene
    stomach
    suspicious
    seditious
    southern
    serenity
    strategic
    serious
    safely
    special
    sailor
    soldier
    supply
    subtle
    sausages
    sophisticated
    significant
    soufflé
    suitable
    screed
    sheer
    sacred
    select
    shield
    said
    service
    suit
    surgeon
    scheme

t. tiny
    taut
    turn
    technique
    trouble

u. universal
    unconscious
    usual
    useful
    usurp
    uniform

v. vitality
    view
    vegetable
    visual
    very
    voice
    vehicle

w. weird
    wasp
    worst
    wrench
    wiry
    watch

y. year
    yearn
    yolk
    yield
    yawn

Finish the story dictations

The following set of short dictations have been used with great success for individual children and groups of two, giving strong motivation to improve their spelling. Constant practice of these dications will help revise basic words, word groupings and endings.

'Stories' of varying length will appear here, but you can make them longer as confidence and accuracy grow. The dictations have been designed to finish on a 'cliff-hanger' - get your child to practise their creative writing by asking them to finish the stories off!

Dictation example:

Jane did not know which direction to take when she came to the crossroads. She had set out early that morning to visit her aunt. It was Wednesday and the shops were shut, so she could not ask the way. She thought she might meet someone and she saw a boy mending a puncture in his bike. He looked up and she found he was a friend from school, who soon told her which way to go. She had a nice tea in her aunt's garden and altogether it was a lovely day.

One Saturday in summer, George and I were at the seaside. We went for a paddle to see how warm the water was. As we were wading into the waves, we both saw a bottle bobbing about in the water. George grabbed it and shook out a message and read what it said. 'Help, I am stranded on the rock and the tide is coming up, please get a boat and help me.'
(Now get your child to finish the story!)

As my mother and I were walking to the station last Wednesday, she said suddenly, 'Oh! Look at that ginger cat up on the tower near the garage.' It was very high up and miaowing loudly. So we missed our train and sent for the fireman and . . .
(Now get your child to finish the story!)

The boys were walking in the forest when a strong wind sprang up. The trees swayed and some branches fell on their heads. Suddenly there was a loud crash and . . .
(Now get your child to finish the story!)

On the other side of the field, I could see a large dark object. I walked over towards it and saw a man lying on the ground near to his crashed aeroplane. As I got near him, he opened his eyes and . . .
(Now get your child to finish the story!)

57

I was going to see my aunt in London. She lives in a busy street in the West End. On the way there, I was looking in a shop window when a man came up behind me. I felt a hand in my pocket. I turned round and he ran off . . . but my purse had gone. I had to think quickly what to do . . .

It was a boiling hot day and I longed for an ice-cold drink. My mother was fussing because an elderly uncle and aunt were coming to tea. I had a swing in the hammock to cool myself down and as I was going to and fro, there was a tearing and a creaking sound and I fell into . . .

The bus stopped at the edge of the grass, near the church. The people got off to see the royal wedding. The princess wore a dress of stiff blue silk but as she was pretty ugly no-one noticed. The carriage brought the prince to the door but as he alighted there was a blinding flash and . . .

When we went for a walk along the cliffs at Dover, we caught sight of a ship in distress out at sea. It was a large cargo boat, listing badly. We told the coastguard and we watched a cutter go out to rescue the crew but . . .

The young dolphin was playing happily in the warm waters of the ocean when suddenly he saw a huge shape ahead of him. As he drew nearer, he saw a small boy sitting on a rock, not far from the wreck and . . .

The road was rough, then he had to cross a ploughed field. He thought he would never reach his friend's house. At last he stood coughing at the door, weary from a trek of many miles. The door was flung open and . . .

David and John went fishing on Saturday and they took their lunch with them. As they were sitting on the bank, David called out, 'I've got a bite', but he fell backwards as he pulled hard on the line. At the final pull, he brought out an old boot! When they looked round a cow had . . .

The boys entered the haunted old castle. Suddenly an owl hooted; they were scared, but they carried on into the Great Hall, which was full of armour. As they walked in, there was a loud crash and . . .

Flash Cards

Cut out the flash cards
that relate to the lesson
you are studying.

rat	mad
rod	cub
can	sit
rot	mat

Lesson 1

Lesson 1

Lesson 1

Lesson 1

Lesson 1

Lesson 1

Lesson 1

Lesson 1

bit	tub
rate	made
rode	cube
cane	site

rote	mate
bite	tube
pine	fine
line	lone

Lesson
1

Lesson
1

Lesson
1

Lesson
1

Lesson
1

Lesson
1

Lesson
1

Lesson
1

cone	done
gone	pane
vane	mane
crane	care

Lesson
1

Lesson
1

Lesson
1

Lesson
1

Lesson
1

Lesson
1

Lesson
1

Lesson
1

dare	stare
bare	bore
wore	store
core	stop

Lesson
1

Lesson
1

Lesson
1

Lesson
1

Lesson
1

Lesson
1

Lesson
1a

Lesson
1

run	tap
bob	sit
stopping	running
tapping	bobbing

Lesson
1a

Lesson
1a

Lesson
1a

Lesson
1a

Lesson
1a

Lesson
1a

Lesson
1a

Lesson
1a

sitting	hope
cane	tape
hoping	caning
taping	hopping

canning	tapping
station	proportion
vocation	ration
suction	fraction

Lesson
1a

Lesson
1a

Lesson
2

Lesson
2

Lesson
2

Lesson
2

Lesson
2

Lesson
2

direction	vacation
adaptation	fiction
motion	lotion
nation	conviction

Lesson

2

Lesson

2

Lesson

2

Lesson

2

Lesson

2

Lesson

2

Lesson

2

Lesson

2

partition	section
erection	adoption
auction	creation
function	portion

Lesson
2

Lesson
2

Lesson
2

Lesson
2

Lesson
2

Lesson
2

Lesson
2

Lesson
2

walk	talk
stalk	miniature
picture	mixture
nature	feature

caricature	posture
capture	overture
fixture	puncture
creature	pasture

furniture	rapture
mature	venture
adventure	palm
calm	psalm

balm	might
sight	light
knight	story
pretty	county

country	bottle
needle	stable
rubble	marble
table	cradle

Lesson
4

Lesson
3

Lesson
4

Lesson
4

Lesson
4

Lesson
4

Lesson
4

Lesson
4

people	enable
ladle	feeble
cable	wheedle
able	muddle

Lesson
4

Lesson
4

Lesson
4

Lesson
4

Lesson
4

Lesson
4

Lesson
4

Lesson
4

rumble	scrabble
bobble	treadle
angle	angel
could	should

would	fright
night	right
fight	money
honey	donkey

Lesson
4

Lesson
4

Lesson
4

Lesson
4

Lesson
4

Lesson
4

Lesson
4

Lesson
4

monkey	city
civic	civil
citizen	citadel
cinema	civility

Lesson 5

Lesson 5

Lesson 5

Lesson 5

Lesson 5

Lesson 5

cine camera	cycle
bicycle	tricycle
cede	recede
precede	concede

Lesson
5

Lesson
5

Lesson
5

Lesson
5

Lesson
5

Lesson
5

Lesson
5

Lesson
5

proceed	ceiling
certain	circus
circle	circular
race	dance

Lesson 5

Lesson 5

Lesson 5

Lesson 5

Lesson 5

Lesson 5

Lesson 5

Lesson 5

office	service
police	defiance
scarce	advice
decide	association

anticipate	old
cold	gold
told	sold
hold	many

any	through
though	thought
throughout	thorough
thoroughfare	enough

Lesson 6

Lesson 5

Lesson 6

Lesson 6

Lesson 6

Lesson 6

Lesson 6

Lesson 6

plough	bough
cough	trough
rough	tough
angel	vessel

Lesson
6

Lesson
6

Lesson
6

Lesson
6

Lesson
6

Lesson
6

Lesson
6

Lesson
6

travel	hotel
barrel	tunnel
heather	feather
leather	weather

Lesson

6

Lesson

6

Lesson

6

Lesson

6

Lesson

6

Lesson

6

Lesson

6

Lesson

6

done	gone
does	goes
beautiful	because
usual	many

Lesson
6

Lesson
6

Lesson
6

Lesson
6

Lesson
7

Lesson
7

Lesson
7

Lesson
7

useful	necessary
disappoint	beautifully
difficult	unusual
any	usefully

Lesson 7

Lesson 7

Lesson 7

Lesson 7

Lesson 7

Lesson 7

Lesson 7

Lesson 7

happened	suddenly
beauty	different
usually	anyhow
use	several

Lesson
7

Lesson
7

Lesson
7

Lesson
7

Lesson
7

Lesson
7

Lesson
7

Lesson
7

opportunity	casual
really	misuse
pleasure	measure
treasure	cruise

Lesson
7

Lesson
7

Lesson
7

Lesson
7

Lesson
7

Lesson
7

Lesson
7

Lesson
7

bruise	who
what	when
whom	whether
whither	whoever

Lesson
8

Lesson
7

Lesson
8

Lesson
8

Lesson
8

Lesson
8

Lesson
8

Lesson
8

whatever	whenever
where	why
but	how
whine	whistle

Lesson 8

Lesson 8

Lesson 8

Lesson 8

Lesson 8

Lesson 8

white	whisper
wheel	while
whisky	whim
smoulder	shoulder

boulder	caught
taught	sausages
gaudy	aunt
Australia	Austria

Lesson
9

Lesson
8

Lesson
9

Lesson
9

Lesson
9

Lesson
9

Lesson
9

Lesson
9

author	autumn
August	laughter
daughter	slaughter
naughty	sauce

Lesson
9

Lesson
9

Lesson
9

Lesson
9

Lesson
9

Lesson
9

Lesson
9

Lesson
9

saucy	raucous
saucer	there
their	father
aunt	uncle

Lesson
9

Lesson
9

Lesson
9

Lesson
9

Lesson
10

Lesson
9

Lesson
10

Lesson
10

niece	nephew
brother	mother
sister	son
daughter	godmother

Lesson

10

Lesson

10

Lesson

10

Lesson

10

Lesson

10

Lesson

10

Lesson

10

Lesson

10

parent	grandpa
neighbour	alien
foreigner	shield
field	wield

Lesson
10

Lesson
10

Lesson
10

Lesson
10

Lesson
10

Lesson
10

Lesson
10

Lesson
10

yield	motor
tractor	factor
proctor	mentor
sailor	major

Lesson
11

Lesson
10

Lesson
11

Lesson
11

Lesson
11

Lesson
11

Lesson
11

Lesson
11

pastor	rector
mirror	doctor
author	terror
ought	bought

Lesson
11

Lesson
11

Lesson
11

Lesson
11

Lesson
11

Lesson
11

Lesson
11

Lesson
11

sought	brought
sulk	hulk
bulk	heart
heard	learn

Lesson
11

Lesson
11

Lesson
11

Lesson
11

Lesson
12

Lesson
11

Lesson
12

Lesson
12

search	beard
earn	fear
dear	rear
pear	near

Lesson
12

Lesson
12

Lesson
12

Lesson
12

Lesson
12

Lesson
12

Lesson
12

Lesson
12

knew	knee
knight	knife
know	knock
knowledge	autumn

Lesson
12

Lesson
12

Lesson
12

Lesson
12

Lesson
12

Lesson
12

Lesson
12

Lesson
12

solemn	column
condemn	comb
bomb	lamb
thumb	plumb

Lesson
12

Lesson
12

Lesson
12

Lesson
12

Lesson
12

Lesson
12

Lesson
12

Lesson
12

crumb	climb
dumb	tomb
succumb	germ
gym	gentle

Lesson
12

Lesson
12

Lesson
12

Lesson
12

Lesson
13

Lesson
12

Lesson
13

Lesson
13

ginger	gist
gender	page
edge	strange
large	advantage

Lesson 13 Lesson 13 Lesson 13 Lesson 13 Lesson 13 Lesson 13 Lesson 13 Lesson 13

damage	arranging
managed	courageous
danger	manager
menagerie	bruise

Lesson
13

Lesson
13

Lesson
13

Lesson
13

Lesson
13

Lesson
13

Lesson
13

Lesson
13

cruise	fruit
suit	build
juice	chord
choir	chemist

Lesson
13

Lesson
13

Lesson
13

Lesson
13

Lesson
14

Lesson
13

Lesson
14

Lesson
14

Christmas	character
chronic	chasm
technical	architect
mechanic	stomach

Lesson 14

Lesson 14

Lesson 14

Lesson 14

Lesson 14

Lesson 14

Lesson 14

Lesson 14

echo	orchestra
scheme	doubt
debt	league
vague	tongue

Lesson
14

Lesson
14

Lesson
14

Lesson
14

Lesson
14

Lesson
14

Lesson
14

Lesson
14

crocus	focus
discus	cactus
famous	enormous
fabulous	numerous

dangerous	various
cautious	mysterious
curious	infectious
miscellaneous	courageous

Lesson
15

Lesson
15

Lesson
15

Lesson
15

Lesson
15

Lesson
15

Lesson
15

Lesson
15

initial	substantial
essential	partial
impartial	industrial
social	racial

Lesson
16

Lesson
16

Lesson
16

Lesson
16

Lesson
16

Lesson
16

Lesson
16

Lesson
16

special	artificial
official	commercial
pretentious	ambitious
superstitious	infectious

Lesson
16

Lesson
16

Lesson
16

Lesson
16

Lesson
16

Lesson
16

Lesson
16

Lesson
16

cautious	conscientious
precious	spacious
delicious	conscious
suspicious	vicious

Lesson
16

Lesson
16

Lesson
16

Lesson
16

Lesson
16

Lesson
16

Lesson
16

Lesson
16

a	a	a	a
a	a	a	a
b	b	b	c
c	c	d	d
d	e	e	e
e	e	e	e
e	f	f	f
g	g	g	h

a	a	a	a
a	a	a	a
c	b	b	b
d	d	d	d
e	e	e	d
e	e	e	e
f	f	f	e
h	g	g	g

h	h	i	i
l	l	l	l
l	l	j	j
j	k	k	k
l	l	l	l
l	l	l	m
m	m	m	m
m	n	n	n

i	i	h	h
i	i	i	i
j	j	i	i
k	k	k	j
l	l	l	l
m	l	l	l
m	m	m	m
n	n	n	m

n	n	n	o
o	o	o	o
o	o	o	p
p	p	q	q
q	r	r	r
r	r	r	r
r	s	s	s
s	s	s	s

o	n	n	n
o	o	o	o
p	o	o	o
q	q	p	p
r	r	r	q
r	r	r	r
s	s	s	r
s	s	s	s

s	t	t	t
t	t	t	t
t	u	u	u
u	u	u	u
u	v	v	v
w	w	w	x
x	x	y	y
y	z	z	z

t	t	t	s
t	t	t	t
u	u	u	t
u	u	u	u
v	v	v	u
x	w	w	w
y	y	x	x
z	z	z	y

Notes

Useful contacts

British Dyslexia Association
BDA National Helpline: 0118 966 8271
Email: helpline@bdadyslexia.org.uk
www.bdadyslexia.org.uk

Dyslexia Action (formerly The Dyslexia Institute)
Tel: 01784 222300
Fax: 01784 222333
Email: info@dyslexiaaction.org.uk
www.dyslexiaaction.org.uk

The Dore Programme
Tel: 0870 880 6060
Email: info@dore.co.uk
www.dore.co.uk

Parent support and information
www.dyslexia-parent.com